BODIES FROM THE BOG

DISCARD

BODIES FROM THE BOG

James M. Deem

HOUGHTON MIFFLIN COMPANY

BOSTON

For David

Copyright © 1998 by James M. Deem

Photo credits:
Pages 26, 29: The British Museum, London
Page 16: W. A. Casparie
Pages 7, 8, 14, 23 (Caergwrle Castle), 25: James M. Deem
Pages 6, 12, 17, 21, 32, 33: Drents Museum, Assen, Netherlands
Pages vi, 1–3, 38: Forhistorisk Museum, Moesgård, Denmark
Pages 9, 13, 31, 37: Landesmuseum, Schleswig, Germany
Pages 24, 28: National Museum of Ireland, Dublin
Page 23 (Caergwrle Bowl): National Museum of Wales, Cardiff
Pages 4, 7, 9, 18, 20, 22, 30: Nationalmuseet, Copenhagen, Denmark
Pages ii, 10, 11, 36: Silkeborg Museum, Silkeborg, Denmark
Page 34: Theo Holleman

Designed by Lisa Diercks
The text of this book is set in Emigre Filosofia.

Library of Congress Cataloging-in-Publication Data
Deem, James M.
　　　Bodies from the bog / James M. Deem.
　　　　　p.　cm.
　　　Summary: Describes the discovery of bog bodies in northern Europe and the evidence that their remains reveal about themselves and the civilizations in which they lived.
　　　RNF ISBN 0-395-85784-8　　　PAP ISBN 0-618-35402-6
　　　1. Bog bodies—Europe—Juvenile literature. 2. Man, Prehistoric—Europe—Juvenile literature. 3. Human remains (Archaeology)—Europe—Juvenile literature. 4. Europe—Antiquities—Juvenile literature. [1. Bog bodies. 2. Prehistoric peoples. 3. Human remains (Archaeology). 4. Europe—Antiquities.]　I. Title.
GN803.D45　1998
569.9—DC21

97-12010
CIP
AC

Printed in Singapore
TWP 10 9 8 7 6

contents

Denmark's Nebelgards Mose, a bog where peat was cut for many years

1. A BODY FROM THE BOG

ON THE LAST SATURDAY OF APRIL 1952, NEAR THE VILLAGE of Grauballe, Denmark, a group of men were digging in a raised bog they had partially drained. They dug past the upper layer of peat moss into a rich layer of compact, dark-brown peat perfect for fuel, their shovels slicing brick-sized chunks. They stacked the peat on the surface. When it dried, it would be burned for heat in a fireplace or furnace.

That afternoon, though, the men made an unexpected discovery. About three feet below the surface their shovels struck the head of a dead man. His eyes were closed, his face partially flattened by the weight of the peat. His skin was as brown as the earth that surrounded him.

The peat cutters quickly reported their find to a local doctor, who wondered if it might not be a "bog body," that is, a type of natural mummy: the preserved body of a person who was buried in the bog perhaps thousands of years ago. A number of such bodies had been found in Denmark, so the doctor called an archaeologist at the nearby Moesgård Museum of Prehistory. The next morning Professor P. V. Glob arrived at the site and examined the body of what has come to be called the Grauballe Man.

Professor Glob directed workers to cut the peat carefully away from

The Grauballe Man, shortly after his discovery in 1952

The Grauballe Man after workers had removed the peat from one side of his body, shortly after his discovery in 1952

one side of the body. Then he sketched the body and photographed it. To make sure that it was safely preserved, he asked workers to construct a crate. Sheets of corrugated metal were driven into the ground beside and under the body so that it could be carried away from the site still encased in its own block of peat.

The peat containing the Grauballe Man was taken to the Museum of Prehistory. There the peat was removed from the body. Because the man's bones had softened so much that they could now be bent, plaster casts of the body were made to ensure that it would be returned to its original position after scientific study.

Next a team of scientists examined the man's body. By inspecting his teeth, they determined that he was in his late thirties at the time of his death. By studying his skin, they found that his hands showed no sign of manual labor, and his fingers were so well preserved that prints could actually be taken from some of them. By searching the body for signs of injuries, they discovered that the man had three wounds, all inflicted about the same time: his skull had been fractured, his throat had been cut, and one of his legs had been broken—perhaps accidentally or even intentionally, maybe to prevent him from running away. By analyzing the contents of his intestines, they learned that he had eaten a watery soup shortly before he died. By studying the seeds and grains in the soup, they realized that some had been contaminated with fungus, which may have acted like a drug, causing him to hallucinate or even to go into a coma after his meal. By checking the growing cycles of the seeds and grains, they discovered an absence of summer or fall fruit. They concluded that he had probably consumed the soup in winter or very early spring.

But who was he? everyone wondered. And why had he been killed?

At first, some residents of Grauballe thought that the body might be that of Red Christian, a peat cutter who had disappeared in 1887 when he was drunk and had never been seen again. But Professor Glob took a revolutionary step and dated the body by using radiocarbon analysis of a small piece of the Grauballe Man's liver: the results suggested that his body had been put into the bog about 55 B.C., during a time period called the Iron Age. The body, Glob proved, couldn't be Red Christian.

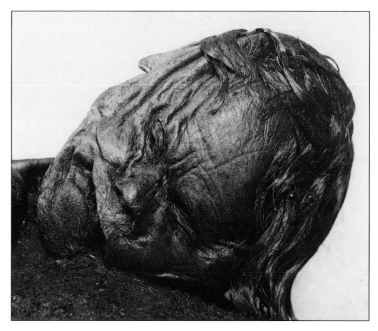

The face of the Grauballe Man before being treated and placed on display in the Moesgård Museum of Prehistory

And he died, Glob concluded, because he was sacrificed. From reading the works of Roman historian Tacitus and other early authors, Glob knew that during the Iron Age the people of northern Europe sometimes practiced human sacrifice. Because the Grauballe Man's hands were uncalloused, he may have been an important member of his society and a more likely candidate for sacrifice. Because he was fed a soup intended to induce drowsiness or a coma, he may have eaten it as part of a ritual. Because his throat was cut, his blood may have been used in a ceremony. And because he died in late winter or early spring, his death may have been an offering to the goddess of spring.

The first photograph ever made of a Danish bog body, 1892

2. A BUNDLE OF BOG BODIES

THE GRAUBALLE MAN WAS NOT THE FIRST BOG BODY EVER discovered. In fact, the earliest written reports of such discoveries come from the 1600s. When these bodies turned up, they were usually reburied, sometimes in cemeteries, sometimes right where they were found. Some bodies were dried and ground into "mummy powder" and sold as medicine. A few bodies, or parts of them, were taken home by their discoverers as additions to their own "antique" collections. At least one was sold at an auction in London. Because of the way they were treated, almost all of the bodies discovered up to the late 1800s no longer exist.

By then, scientists began to take an interest in bog bodies. They studied them and their clothing; guesses were made about the reasons for their deaths. A few were put on display in museums, generally as curiosities. A German scientist named Alfred Dieck even tried to compile a list of all the bog bodies ever found. After fifty years of work, he was able to record about 1,850 cases. Unfortunately, many of these are no more than "paper" bog bodies—that is, bodies that were mentioned in newspaper articles and other written accounts. Because these bodies were "discovered" long ago and never saved, they may never have really existed. That may explain why many paper bog bodies are much more dramatic than the bodies that have been found and studied. For

The Ages of Bog Bodies

When talking about the time periods of prehistory, archaeologists refer to them by Age. Although they vary by country, here are the five most common Ages when people who became bog bodies lived:

Neolithic Age
4500 B.C. to 2000 B.C.

Bronze Age
2000 B.C. to 800 B.C.

Iron Age
800 B.C. to 0

Roman period
0 to A.D. 400

Middle Ages
A.D. 400 to A.D. 1500

Traditionally, peat cutters (here in the Netherlands in the early part of the twentieth century) drain part of a bog and shovel the peat in chunks, called mumps. Such close contact enabled peat cutters to discover many bog bodies as well as objects.

Wheelbarrows were used to transport the dried peat out of the bog.

As each mump was cut, the worker stacked the peat nearby and left it there until dry.

example, one paper account reported that the body of a spear-holding female warrior, killed by arrows, had been found in Germany in 1906. Near her were the bodies of six men, all shot by arrows and slashed with swords. Scientists doubt that such a startling discovery was ever made.

Most scientists were much more interested in real, not paper, bog bodies. In the six years before the Grauballe Man was discovered, a series of bog bodies were found. This time, however, archaeologists and other scientists were ready to study the finds.

In 1946, the skeleton of a thirty-five- to forty-year-old man was found in the Porsmose Bog near Naestved, Denmark. He had been

The skull of the Porsmose Man

killed by arrows in about 3500 B.C. One arrowhead pierced his nose and mouth, but this shot did not kill him. Instead, he was mortally wounded by an arrow that went through his breastbone into his aorta.

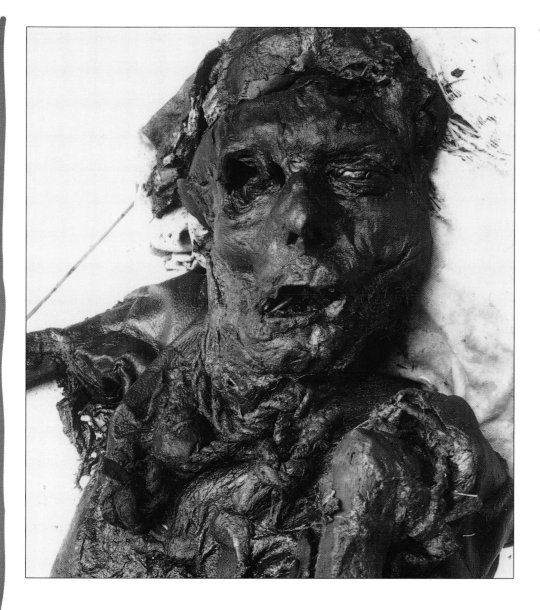

The Borremose Man, discovered in 1946, showed signs of a violent death.

. Also in 1946, a 2,500-year-old bog body was found in Borremose, Denmark. The next year, another was uncovered in the same bog. And in 1948 a third body was discovered there. The first two showed signs

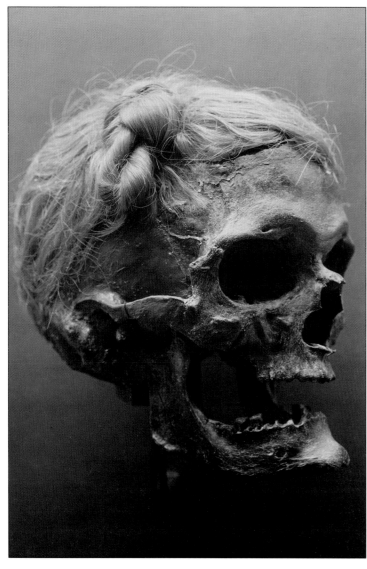
The Osterby Head with its striking Swabian knot

of a violent death. Because they were found over a half-mile area, scientists doubted that their deaths were related. When the local museum curator sent the third body to the National Museum in Copenhagen, he included a note that read, "I have great pleasure in sending you the customary annual bog body."

In May 1948, a grisly discovery was made near Osterby, Germany. Two peat cutters uncovered a human head wrapped in a deerskin cape. Although the men looked for the rest of the body, they could not find it. Scientists concluded that the Osterby Head had been deposited in the bog by itself and had belonged to a man about fifty or sixty years old. Only a small amount of skin remained on the skull, but what intrigued the scientists was his hairstyle: the Osterby Head displayed a Swabian knot, a figure-eight twist held without any fasteners. The Swabians were a group of German tribes of 2,000 years ago who wore their hair in such a fashion.

In 1950, about eleven miles from Grauballe, a bog body that is still considered the best preserved was unearthed. Called Tollund Man for the bog in which he was found, he was so fresh-looking that peat cutters called the police; they were certain they had stumbled across a murder victim. It turned out that he had been lying in the bog about 2,000 years. And although he looked as peaceful and calm as if

The Tollund Man had been hanged

Despite the circumstances of his death, the face of the Tollund Man is still peaceful and at rest.

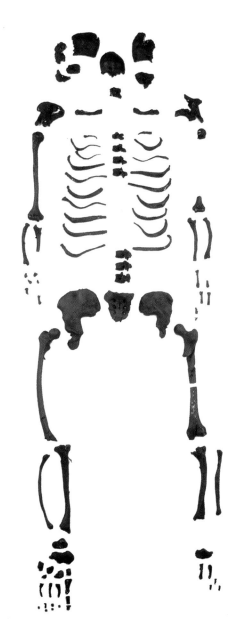

he were sleeping, a plaited cord around his neck showed that he had probably been hanged.

In 1951, Dutch peat cutters discovered the body of the Zweeloo Woman. Her "body" consisted of a skeleton, along with skin and intestines. Her skeleton revealed a rare condition: the bones from her elbows to her wrists and from her knees to her ankles were very short. Her arms and legs would have looked unusual; she may have had difficulty walking. The contents of her intestines showed that she had eaten a gruel made from millet and a few blackberries shortly before she died.

And in May 1952, about a month after the Grauballe Man was found, the bodies of a man and a fourteen-year-old girl were found in a bog near Schleswig, Germany. Scientists don't know if their bodies were deposited in the peat at the same time but the man's body was pegged down with eight stakes, and the girl had been blindfolded with

The skeleton (*above*) and skin (*right*) of the Zweeloo Woman

12

a woolen headband and a large stone had been placed beside her. Scientists could not find any signs of violence on the girl's body, but they believed that the man may have been strangled by a thin hazel rod, which had been wound around his neck.

No matter how these people died, their bodies would have decayed and never been seen again once they were buried, except that something amazing happened in their cold watery bog graves, something that allowed them to tell the stories of their deaths.

Early Europeans considered watery sites to be magical places where people could communicate with the supernatural world. Here, reeds grow around a shallow lake that one day may become a fen.

3. THE LIFE OF A BOG

EARLY PEOPLE OF EUROPE BELIEVED THAT WATERY PLACES were quite special. They thought they could communicate with the supernatural world there—gods and goddesses and even their dead ancestors. Sometimes they deposited weapons, tools, jewelry, and other objects in these wetlands to please or thank their gods. And sometimes they placed sacrificed human bodies there.

Although some ancient objects have been found on the bottom of European rivers and lakes, some have also been unearthed by farmers and peat cutters who were working in peat-filled soil.

Peat is found in waterlogged areas called fens and bogs. It is a soil that is composed of partially decayed dead plants which have piled on top of each other for thousands of years. Fens are created when shallow lakes lose their water supply and become stagnant pools. Reeds growing around the edge die and begin to fill in the pool. Because the pool is waterlogged, the reeds decay slowly and over time build up layers of fen peat.

Bogs are created if sphagnum moss begins to grow in a fen. This moss which lives on rainwater builds up its own layers of peat on top of the fen peat. A thin layer of moss and other hardy plants live on top of the bog, like a bumpy floating carpet, dotted with occasional pools of water. Underneath it lies the bog peat, which is 90 percent water.

The Magic of Sphagnum Moss

Early European civilizations knew that sphagnum moss had special qualities. By 1200 B.C., wounds were treated with bandages made from dried sphagnum moss. Even during World War I, such bandages were used on the European battlefield when cotton bandages were in short supply. And bog water from sphagnum peat bogs was taken by sailors on long sea voyages because it stayed fresher much longer than spring or well water. Even in gardening, sphagnum peat moss never becomes moldy or bug-infested.

The Esterweger Bog in Northern Germany. Pools of water are often part of a bog.

When something is placed into the bog, an object or a body, it is immersed in watery peat.

Although fen peat and bog peat preserve objects equally well, they differ in their preservation of human remains. Fen peat, for example, allows bacteria to thrive. This in turn promotes the decay of a body placed in fen peat.

Bog peat produces quite different results. Scientists discovered that sphagnan, a substance in sphagnum moss, prevents the growth of microbes. When a body is placed in bog peat, sphagnan prevents bacteria from growing and the body can become mummified. Even wooden objects placed into a peat bog are preserved from rot for the same reason. However, any material made from a plant product (such as linen cloth) will decay over time and disappear without a trace. That may explain why Tollund Man was discovered wearing only a leather cap and belt. His linen clothing may simply have deteriorated in the bog.

Scientists have also learned that sphagnan tans a body, turning it into a kind of leather. But unlike normal leather with its brownish tint, many bog bodies develop a much darker "black coffee" color. In a few unusual cases, the internal organs of a bog body have become tanned while the skin has decayed. At least one scientist, T. J. Painter, believes that this happened when the person had been the victim of a fire—perhaps burned at the stake as a witch.

But a body cannot be preserved in a peat bog unless one final condition is met: it would have to be placed in the soggy bog almost immediately after death and remain covered with bog water. This avoids two problems. First, scavenging animals will not smell the scent of the body and attack it. Second, the body will not come into contact with oxygen, assuring its preservation. This process shows how remarkable bog bodies truly are.

Whether bodies become skeletons in fen peat or mummies in bog peat, scientists refer to both as "bog bodies." But not all bog mummies are preserved equally well, even when the bacteria are thwarted and the skin is tanned. Some, like Tollund Man and Grauballe Man, have been so well preserved that, at a glance, they look quite lifelike. However, despite their outward appearance, many of their internal organs are decayed and their bones decalcified. Parts of some bog mummies have decayed, perhaps because of their position in the peat; the side facing down is often preserved better. Other bog bodies have been so flattened by the peat pressing against them that they are much harder to study, for there is nothing to examine except skin and hair.

Whatever their condition, they provide scientists with valuable information about persons who lived and died long ago.

Although technically a bog mummy, the Emmer-Erfscheidenveen Man has few remains.

The silver Gundestrup Cauldron, about two feet in diameter,
may have been used as part of a sacrificial ceremony.

4. Magic Cauldrons and More

ALTHOUGH BOG BODIES ARE THE MOST DRAMATIC DIS-coveries made in peat bogs, many of the objects that early Europeans deposited in watery places are equally fascinating. They provide a glimpse of the customs and beliefs of civilizations that flourished thousands of years ago.

Here are a few important finds made in bogs and fens:

The Gundestrup Cauldron (Denmark). Found in 1891 in Raeve Bog, near the bog where the three Borremose bodies were later unearthed, the Gundestrup Cauldron is one of the most important bog discoveries ever. The silver cauldron was deliberately broken into pieces and placed on the surface of the bog. Years later, sphagnum moss overgrew it. When it was found, the cauldron lay almost two feet below the surface.

The cauldron is remarkable for the scenes depicted around the bowl, both inside and out. One inner panel appears to show the ritual of human sacrifice. Although scientists will never know for certain what this illustrates, some have offered the following possibility: A lower row of warriors, perhaps prisoners of war, march toward a representation of a cauldron. A larger individual holds one warrior upside down over the cauldron, collecting his blood. Then, on the top row, a

The sacrificial panel of
the Gundestrup Cauldron

line of warriors ride away from the cauldron, after their sacrifice, to their afterlife. The killing of the prisoners may have been an attempt to please or thank the gods; it may also have been a way to determine what the future would bring (sometimes the internal organs of the sacrificed prisoners were studied).

Scientists have concluded that the cauldron was made in southeastern Europe about 150 B.C. by as many as five different silversmiths. No one knows how it came to Denmark, whether as a present to an important chief or as the spoils of war. However it got there, it was obviously the most valuable object an important member of the tribe could have possessed. Destroying it and leaving it as an offering in Raeve Bog shows how desperate the tribe may have become to bring about better times.

Many other ancient cauldrons have been discovered in bogs, but none has been as decorated as the Gundestrup Cauldron.

The Dejbjerg Wagons (Denmark). Parts of two unusual wagons, about 2,100 years old, were found in Dejbjerg Bog in the 1880s. They had been taken apart before they were placed in the bog, so researchers were able to rebuild one of the wagons, using the pieces that they had found. Because the wagons were decorated with bronze parts as well as human masks, scientists believe that the wagons were used in an important ceremony, not by an ordinary farmer.

Tacitus, who wrote about tribes living in what is now Germany and Denmark, described a ceremony for a goddess called Nerthus, or Mother Earth. According to Tacitus, she toured the land in her wagon, bringing happiness to those she visited. Then she was taken to a lake where she was washed by servants. Afterward the servants were swallowed by the lake,

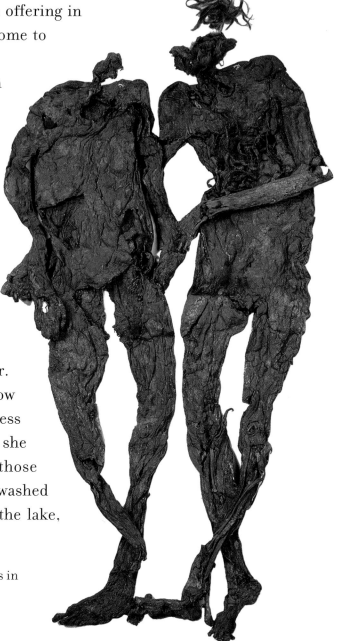

The Weerdinge Men, two flattened bog bodies found in the Netherlands in 1904. Notice that the intestines of the man on the right are lying on his chest, exactly as the discoverers found them. Did the people who killed them try to foretell the future through his intestines?

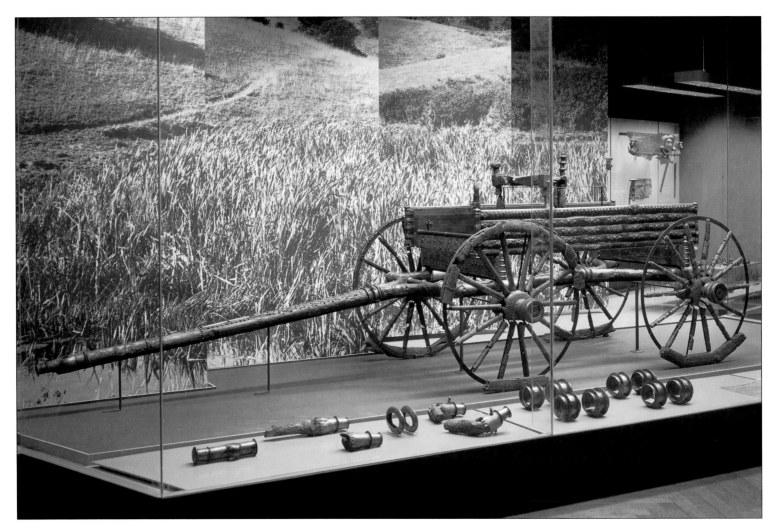

The Dejbjerg Wagon, which may
have been used in ceremonies
celebrating Mother Earth

apparently sacrificed. Because the Dejbjerg Wagons were so well decorated and because there was a ceremonial seat, which would hold only
one person, some scientists have connected them to the ceremony
Tacitus describes. However, no human remains were ever recovered
from the Dejbjerg Bog.

The Caergwrle Bowl from Wales. Notice that the top band of gold has a series of sun disks engraved or stamped into it. Scientists believe that these may represent shields hung on the boat's gunwales.

The ruins of Caergwrle Castle

The Caergwrle Bowl (Wales). In a peat bog near Caergwrle Castle, a prehistoric model boat was apparently offered to the gods. Now known as the Caergwrle Bowl, it is 3,000 years old and was thought to be made of oak when it was first found in the 1820s. A more recent look at the bowl has shown scientists that it was carved from stone, decorated with gold leaf. The sides of the bowl show a band of gold near the lip, which is covered with disk-shaped designs. Beneath these are a series of thin triangles, thought to represent oars, and zigzagging lines that many scientists interpret as waves. On the underside of the bowl are long rectangles, perhaps the ribs of a boat, and two eyes like those that are still painted on the bottom of some boats today to ward off evil.

Scientists can only guess why it was deposited in the bog. Probably an important member of the tribe left it, asking in exchange for favorable weather for sailing or good fortune in general. It may have also been left as thanks for a victory.

La Tène Art (Northern Europe). Among the most beautiful items found in bogs are golden neck ornaments called collars or torques. From about 500 B.C., the La Tène Celts began to spread across Europe, eventually making their way to England and Ireland. In the end, the Romans conquered the Celts, but their artwork, as shown in their jewelry and other objects, was deposited in European wetlands to be discovered by farmers, peat cutters, and archaeologists.

One collar, which was made in Germany in about 300 B.C., was deposited in a bog at Knock, County Roscommon. It shows the type of designs developed by La Tène artists: *S*-shaped scrolls, vines, leaves, and spirals. It was most likely worn by a Celtic warrior, and is called the Clonmacnoise collar after the bog in which it was discovered.

The golden collar from Knock, Ireland, is an example of La Tène art.

Flag Fen (England). By far the largest wetland discovery has been what archaeologists at first thought was an entire village.

Called Flag Fen, the "village" was thought to be located on a large artificial island built in the middle of a fen near Peterborough, England. Archaeologists dated wood on the island to between 1363 B.C. and 967 B.C. They expected to find remains of houses under the fen peat that covered the island, believing that the Bronze Age men and women had first built the island and then lived on it.

The people who used Flag Fen lived in round houses with sod roofs. This house has been reconstructed near Flag Fen.

Instead they discovered two wooden walkways linking the island to drier ground. And in the marshy area on the south side of the walkways they found a huge assortment of metal artifacts: about 300 swords, knives, helmets, tools, pins, rings, brooches—most of them broken or bent. Archaeologists know that when offerings were made, the objects were almost always destroyed as a part of the offering. Flag Fen, they concluded, was not a settlement. Rather, the island was built in the fen as a sacred site where people made offerings.

It was also the site of a few burials; the skeletons of seven dogs were found, along with parts of three humans. At least some of the dogs were probably sacrificed. One had been pierced by a wooden stake.

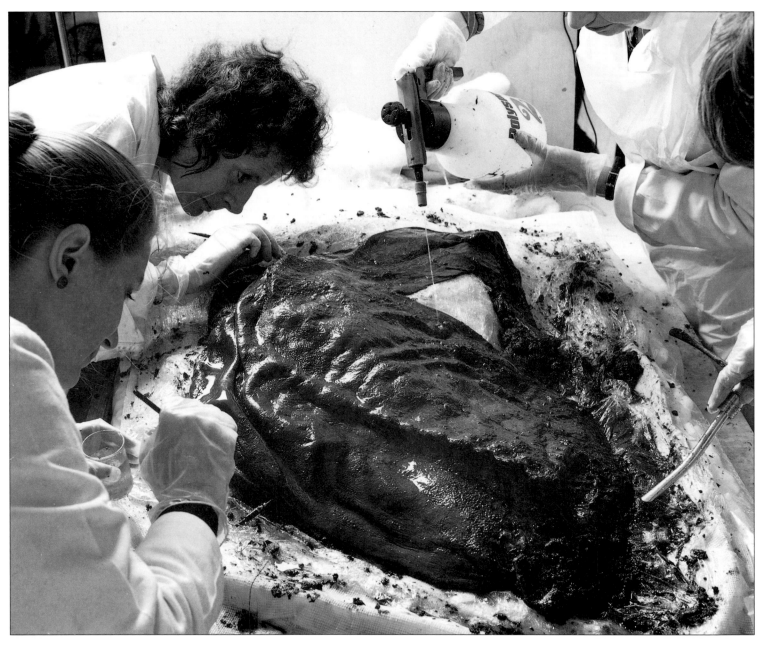

Scientists examine the body of the Lindow Man II, discovered in England in 1984.

5. THE PUZZLE OF BOG BODIES

EVERY BOG BODY IS A SCIENTIFIC PUZZLE. RESEARCHERS must determine when and how the person died. Neither is an easy task. Scientists cannot always say with certainty whether a bog body is male or female. For example, the Windeby Girl (pp. 13, 37) was reexamined by a scientist in 1970 who wondered whether she might actually be a boy. Although still referred to as the Windeby *Girl*, so little remains of the body that no one can prove this is true. And the Weerdinge Men (pp. 21, 37) were thought to be a man and a woman for almost a hundred years before they were reexamined and found to be two men. They may even be father and son, but no one will ever know since the peat that preserves bodies so well also appears to destroy all traces of DNA, which shows the genetic makeup of an individual.

Scientists also want to know why these people died. Were they victims of human sacrifice? Because many bog bodies appear to have been victims of violence and because some have had their throats cut, perhaps as depicted on the Gundestrup Cauldron, many scientists suspect that this is the case. Still, proving that a bog body was sacrificed, rather than murdered or executed, is impossible, but scientists try to support this idea in at least three ways.

First, they attempt to date the body. The approximate year that the person died provides a clue about the possibility of sacrifice.

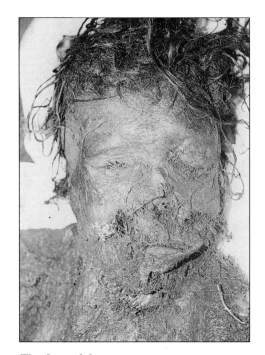

The face of the
Meenybradden Woman

Researchers believe that early European peoples did not conduct human sacrifices. But later peoples did, especially between 500 B.C. and 400 A.D., a time span during which a number of people were buried in the bogs. Occasional human sacrifice continued in parts of northern Europe through the early Middle Ages.

Unfortunately, dating a body is not always easy. A recent Irish body, the Meenybradden Woman, illustrates this. Radiocarbon analysis revealed that the body was probably from the Middle Ages, about 1200 A.D. But the cloak she was wrapped in did not resemble any other cloak from that period. In fact, clothing experts dated it to about the 1700s. How could the Meenybradden Woman have died five hundred years before her cloak was made? Was the radiocarbon analysis mistaken, or were the clothing experts wrong? Or could she have died in 1200, only to be rediscovered in the 1700s, wrapped in a cloak, and reburied? Many think that the science of radiocarbon analysis is far from exact. But no one knows the truth about the Meenybradden Woman yet.

Second, scientists try to determine the season of death. If most bog bodies were sacrifices, it would make sense that they were killed at a certain time of year as part of an annual ritual. The season can be determined by analyzing the contents of their stomachs and intestines. Unfortunately, most bog bodies were found and destroyed long before any scientific study could take place. Few of the surviving bodies have intestines to examine. As a result, only twelve bodies have been studied this way, and their analysis does not point to any pattern.

Finally, scientists attempt to pinpoint the cause of death. This is usually only possible with bog mummies, not skeletons. A skeleton doesn't reveal many secrets about its death because there are no soft

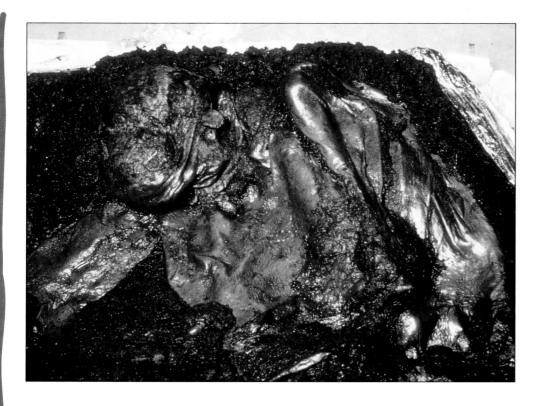

The contents of the Lindow Man II's stomach suggest that he was killed in late winter or early spring.

tissues to retain clues. For example, if the Grauballe Man had been a bog skeleton, scientists would never have known that his throat was cut because such a wound would not have been apparent on his bones. When bog bodies show signs of violence, especially strangulation or cut throats, many scientists argue that this supports the idea of human sacrifice.

A few scientists, however, have offered different reasons why people may have died in the bogs. A person may have been:

• *A condemned criminal.* A criminal may have been hanged and dragged by the neck to the bog. If the trip was long enough, the head could

The Borremose Woman: Was she
sacrificed or did she drown?

easily have become detached from the body. A body in this case might look as if it was sacrificed when it was really hanged.

- *A drowning victim.* A drowning person might have sunk up to her neck in the watery bog. A would-be rescuer might then place a belt or rope around the person's neck, trying in vain to pull her out, causing serious neck injuries in the process. For example, the body of a woman found in Borremose was generally thought to be a victim of sacrifice because of her wounds. But she might have been a drowning victim, according to the scientist C. S. Briggs. As her body slowly sunk into the spongy peat, her head may have remained on the surface long enough for birds and other scavengers to peck or paw at it, causing her head injuries.

- *A wiedergänger.* German folklore has pointed a few researchers toward another explanation. Some people, such as criminals or suicide victims, were thought to become *wiedergängers,* a kind of zombie. To make sure that they would never walk the earth again, their bodies were often mutilated after death and eventually buried in a bog, held down with stakes. This may be the case with the body of a thirty-year-old man and his severed head found near Dätgen, Germany. The body had been damaged after death and the head was pinned down with stakes. Since so much violence was inflicted upon the body, the archaeologist K. W. Struve concluded that the person was a *wiedergänger.*

Despite these alternatives, many scientists believe that most people

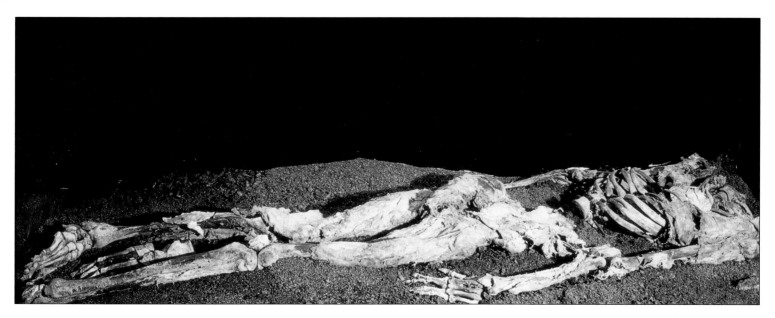

found in the bog were sacrificed. The Dutch archaeologist Wijnand van der Sanden is convinced of this, especially because the bodies were found in watery places (where offerings were made). Some may have been innocent individuals, like children. Others may have been prisoners of war who were killed to thank the gods. Still others may have been physically handicapped or unusual in some way.

The Yde Girl from the Netherlands fits into this latter category. As a worker dredged peat from a small bog near Yde in 1897, he pulled up the body of a sixteen-year-old girl. He was so frightened that he ran away, convinced that this red-haired body was the Devil. Only later, when the body was examined, did scientists realize that the Yde Girl had died 2,000 years earlier. She had scoliosis, a mild spinal curvature that may have affected the way she walked; the toes of her right foot showed signs that she may have been slightly pigeon-toed on this

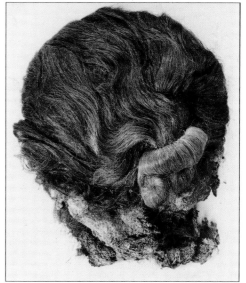

The body and head of the Dätgen Man have produced controversy. Was he sacrificed or was he a *wiedergänger*?

The Yde Girl, as displayed in the Drents Museum

Facing page: The face of the Yde Girl, as it might have looked when she was alive, as reconstructed by an artist

side. Did this mark her as an un-desirable person in her society? No one knows, but her head was shaved on the right side prior to her death. Was this part of a sacrificial ritual, or a punish-ment for a criminal condemned to death? Whichever it was, the Yde Girl was stabbed, strangled with her plaited belt, then de-posited in the bog.

Although her face is now quite gruesome to look at, van der Sanden wanted to know what she might have looked like before she died. A CT-scan of the girl's head allowed researchers to create a three-dimensional model of her skull. Then a medical illustrator went to work, adding soft tissues, skin made of wax, glass eyes, and finally a wig. The final result is quite a different Yde Girl, perhaps the way she'd prefer to be remembered.

Bog Body Solves Murder

Although bog bodies are mysteries, one body solved a real murder mystery. In 1983 a skull was found in a bog near Manchester, England. Investigators determined that the skull was female, and police, who did not know its age and never suspected that it was part of a bog body, wondered if it belonged to a missing woman. She and her husband had lived near the bog, and her husband had bragged that he had killed his wife and buried her in his garden. When the police showed the skull to the man, he broke down and confessed. Only then, when the man was in jail and awaiting trial, did authorities discover that the skull was 1,700 years old—and male! Even so, the man was convicted on the basis of his confession.

Peat cutting is highly mechanized in countries like Ireland where it is still permitted.
This machine not only cuts the peat but moves it by conveyor belt to a waiting truck.

6. A FINAL DEATH

COMPARED TO EGYPTIAN MUMMIES, WHICH SCIENTISTS estimate to have numbered in the millions, few bog bodies still exist. Researchers can say that, since the 1600s, only 93 verifiable bodies were reported in all of England and Wales. Of these, only 52 have survived to the present; only four are bog mummies. Even then, one of the mummies is simply hair and fingernails. In the Netherlands, 56 bog bodies have been documented, but only 13 of these have survived, either as mummies or skeletons; the rest exist only on paper. And scientists in Denmark or Germany cannot even say how many bodies have been found in their countries because such poor records have been kept.

The one thing that scientists do know is that very few, if any, new bog bodies will turn up in the future. The last body discovered in England was Lindow Man III in 1987, the last in Ireland was found in 1978, and the last body found in Denmark was the Grauballe Man in 1952.

More and more, people wish to preserve the vanishing peat lands of northern Europe since bogs no longer cover the landscape as they once did. In the Netherlands and Denmark, for example, only about one percent of the bog land still exists; peat cutting is no longer allowed there.

In Ireland, where many bog bodies have been found, bogs still

The Tollund Man on display in the Silkeborg Museum. Only his head and feet remain well preserved.

blanket seventeen percent of the country. There, and in England and Germany, peat is still cut, although few peat cutters work there. Instead, peat companies use mechanical diggers to work the bogs. Even if a bog body turned up, no human workers would spot it, at least not before it was cut into pieces. When Lindow Man III was unearthed in England in 1987, it had been chopped into seventy pieces before it was spotted and rescued.

Scientists who want to study bog bodies can turn only to the past. They must reexamine the bodies that have been preserved in museums

The Windeby Girl on display in the Landesmuseum in Schleswig, Germany. A new scientific study of her may help scientists solve some of the mysteries still surrounding her death.

to determine if any new information can be learned. Some like Lindow Man II in the British Museum lie in sterile glass boxes in the middle of crowded museum floors. Some are placed in dioramas like animals in a natural history museum. Others lie in quiet, darkened rooms, waiting for people to pay their final respects. Tollund Man, the Weerdinge Men, and the Yde Girl are in such peaceful circumstances. Others, though, are in storage—sometimes under ideal conditions, sometimes in museum basements next to hot radiators, crumbling to dust. A few that are said to exist cannot even be found.

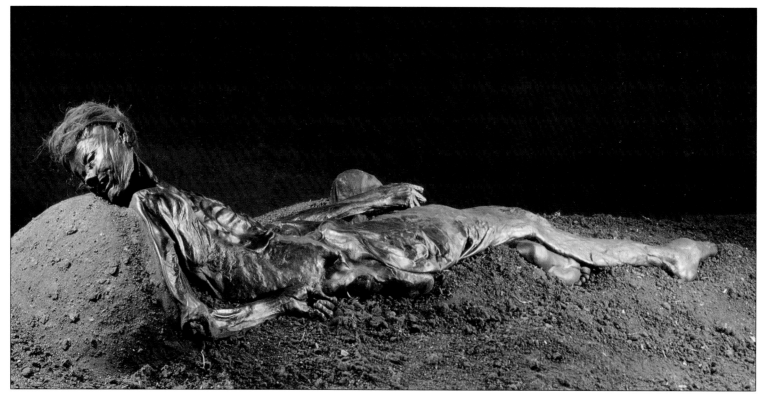

The Grauballe Man on display in the Moesgård Museum near Aarhus, Denmark. As a result of the process used to preserve him after his discovery, his skin became much tighter. Some scientists are still hopeful that even the Grauballe Man can be reexamined in the future.

With new tests and procedures, with determination and perhaps some luck, scientists may still unravel some of the mysteries of bog bodies before they turn to dust. The Grauballe Man and others like him may indeed die a second death, closing one of the few windows that science has to the past.

ACKNOWLEDGMENTS AND BIBLIOGRAPHY

My search for information about bog bodies took me to almost all museums where they are exhibited. Along the way, I met many people who shared information with me. I especially wish to thank Dr. Wijnand A. B. van der Sanden of the Drents Museum in the Netherlands who answered more than his share of questions and made many suggestions after reading a draft of this book. He is perhaps the most knowledgeable person studying bog bodies today, and his book, *Through Nature to Eternity: The Bog Bodies of Northwest Europe* (Amsterdam: Batavian Lion International, 1996), is the most comprehensive source of information and photographs on the subject to date.

In addition to Dr. van der Sanden's book and guidebooks published by the museums that displayed the bodies, the following books and periodicals were helpful to me in my research:

Aldhouse-Green, Stephen (ed.). *Art, Ritual, and Death in Prehistory.* Cardiff: National Museum of Wales, 1996.

Brothwell, Don. *The Bogman and the Archaeology of People.* Cambridge, Massachusetts: Harvard University Press, 1986.

Cockburn, Aidan and Eve. *Mummies, Disease, and Ancient Cultures.* Cambridge, England: Cambridge University Press, 1980.

Dugan, Patrick (ed.). *Wetlands in Danger.* New York: Oxford University Press, 1993.

Fagan, Brian M. (ed.). *The Oxford Companion to Archaeology.* New York: Oxford University Press, 1996.

Glob, P. V. *The Bog People.* Translated by Rupert Bruce-Mitford. London: Faber and Faber, 1969. Reprinted 1988.

Jordan, Paul. *The Face of the Past.* London: Batsford, 1984.

Kelly, Eammon P. *Early Celtic Art in Ireland.* Dublin: National Museum of Ireland, 1993.

Pryor, Francis. *Flag Fen.* London: Batsford/English Heritage, 1991.

Raftery, Barry. *Pagan Celtic Ireland.* New York: Thames and Hudson, 1994.

Ryan, Michael (ed.). *Irish Archaeology Illustrated.* Dublin: Country House, 1994.

Turner, R. C., and R. G. Scaife (eds.). *Bog Bodies: New Discoveries and New Perspectives.* London: British Museum Press, 1995.

index